March of America Facsimile Series

Number 17

Prosperous Voyage

James Rosier

Prosperous Voyage

by James Rosier

ANN ARBOR

UNIVERSITY MICROFILMS, INC.

A Subsidiary of Xerox Corporation

Foreword

*A True Relation of the most prosperous voyage made...
by Captaine George Waymouth...Written by James Rosier*
(London, 1605) describes an exploration of the New England coastal area for a suitable place for settlement. The
sponsors of the voyage, Thomas Arundell, Baron Arundell
of Wardour, and Henry Wriothesley, third Earl of South-
ampton, had been encouraged by earlier narratives to seek
a place in New England to plant a colony. James Rosier, who
had been with Captain Gosnold's expedition of 1602, may
have been a Catholic priest. He took careful note that there
were no crosses, evidence of visitation by Christians, in all
the territory they explored and avoided giving any details
as to latitude. King James was anxious not to offend Spain
by encroaching on land to which they might lay prior claim.

Captain George Waymouth was an experienced seaman
from Devonshire and had made a voyage in search of the
Northwest Passage in 1602. The present expedition sailed
from Dartmouth in March, 1605, and sighted land near
Nantucket about the middle of May, rather farther south
than their goal. They then sailed north to Maine, where
they anchored at Monhegan Island and explored the St.
George and Kennebec rivers. Rosier described the latter as
surpassing the greatest rivers that any of the company had
seen for convenient harborage and the beauty and fertility
of the adjoining land. He was reluctant to praise it beyond
the Thames, but finally declared: "I would boldly affirme it
to be the most rich, beautifull, large and secure harbouring
river that the world affordeth."

Rosier noted abundant timber trees, some large enough to make masts for 400-ton ships, and commented on the fine turpentine issuing from the firs. Other valuable trees and several varieties of fruits were plentiful, and the soil was fertile. There were quantities of fish and shellfish, and pearls were found in large mussels. All in all, Rosier felt that the party had found a land "whose pleasant fertility bewraieth it selfe to be the garden of nature, wherin she only intended to delight hir selfe, having hitherto obscured it to any, except to a purblind generation."

The "purblind generation"—Indians of the Kennebec tribe —were friendly and intelligent, enough so that the explorers had some ado to capture five of them to take to England. When they had accomplished this, Waymouth felt that they had sufficient information to return to England.

Arundell in the meantime had been appointed colonel of one of Archduke Albert's English regiments in the Low Countries and dropped his interest in colonization. The captured Indians, however, were given to Sir John Popham, the Lord Chief Justice, and Sir Ferdinando Gorges. In 1606 Popham and Gorges, armed with the King's patent constituting the Plymouth Company, financed another exploratory voyage, which resulted in 1607 in the Popham colony, the first serious attempt to settle New England.

Annotated reprints of Rosier's *Relation* appear in Henry S. Burrage, ed., *Early English and French Voyages* (New York, 1906) and Charles H. Levermore, ed., *Forerunners and Competitors of the Pilgrims and Puritans* (Brooklyn, 1912).

Prosperous Voyage

A

TRVE RELATION

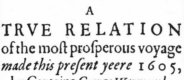

of the moſt proſperous voyage
made this preſent yeere 1605,
by Captaine *George Waymouth,*
in the Diſcouery of the land
of *Virginia:*

Where he diſcouered 60 miles vp
a moſt excellent Riuer; together with a moſt
fertile land.

Written by IAMES ROSIER.
*a Gentleman employed
in the voyage.*

LONDINI
Impenſis GEOR. BISHOP.
1605.

TO THE READER.

BEing employed in this Voyage by the right honourable *Thomas Arundell* Baron of *Warder*, to take due notice, and make true report of the diſcouery therein performed: I became very diligent to obſerue (as much as I could) whatſoeuer was materiall or of conſequence in the buſineſſe, which I collected into this briefe ſumme, intending vpon our returne to publiſh the ſame. But he ſoone changed the courſe of his intendments; and long before our arriuall in *England* had ſo farre engaged himſelfe with the Archduke, that he was conſtrained to relinquiſh this action. But the commodities and profits of the countrey, together with the fitneſſe of plantation, being by ſome honourable Gentlemen of good woorth and qualitie, and Merchants of good ſufficiency and iudgement duly conſidered, haue at their owne charge (intending both their priuate and the common benefit of their countrey) vndertaken the tranſporting of a Colony for the plantation thereof; being much encouraged thereunto by the gracious fauour

TO THE READER.

of the KINGS MAIESTY himselfe, and diuers Lords
of his Highnesse most Honourable Priuie Councell.
After these purposed designes were concluded, I was a-
nimated to publish this briefe Relation, and not before;
because some forrein Nation (being fully assured of the
fruitfulnesse of the countrie) haue hoped hereby to gaine
some knowledge of the place, seeing they could not allure our Captaine or any speciall man of our Company
to combine with them for their direction, nor obtaine
their purpose, in conueying away our Saluages, which
was busily in practise. And this is the cause that I haue
neither written of the latitude or variation most exactly
obserued by our Captaine with sundrie instruments,
which together with his perfect Geographicall Map of
the countrey, he entendeth hereafter to set forth. I haue
likewise purposedly omitted here to adde a collection of
many words in their language to the number of foure or
fiue hundred, as also the names of diuers of their gouernours, aswell their friends as their enemies; being reser-
ued to be made knowen for the benefit of those that shal
goe in the next Voyage. But our particular proceedings
in the whole Discouerie, the commodious situation of
the Riuer, the fertilitie of the land, with the profits there
to be had, and here reported, I refer to be verified by the
whole Company, as being eye-witnesses of my words,
and most of them neere inhabitants vpon the *Thames*.
So with my prayers to God for the conuersion of so ingenious and well disposed people, and for the prosperous successiue euents of the noble intenders the prose-
cution thereof, I rest.

Your friend I. R.

A TRVE RELATION

of *Captaine George Waymouth* his
Voyage, made this present yeere
1 6 0 5 : *in the Discouerie of*
the North part of
Virginia.

Pon Tuesday the 5 day of March,
about ten a clocke afore none, we
set saile from Ratcliffe, and came
to an anker that tide about two a
clocke before Grauesend.

From thence the 10 of March
being Sunday at night we ankered in the Downes: and there rode
til the next day about three a clocke
after none, when with a scant winde we set saile; and by
reason the winde continued Southwardly, we were bea-
ten vp and downe : but on Saturday the 16 day about
foure a clocke after non we put into Dartmouth Hauen,
where the continuance of the winde at South & South-
west constrained vs to ride till the last of this moneth.
There we shipped some of our men, and supplied necessaries for our Ship and Voyage.

Upon Easter day, being the last of March, the winde
comming at North-North-East, about fiue a clocke after none we wayed anker, and put to sea, In the name
of God, being well victualled and furnished with mu-
nition and all necessaries : Our whole Company being but 29 persons ; of whom I may boldly say, few voy-

Vpon Easter
day we put
to sea.

Our Compa-
nie 29 per-
sons.

A 3   ages

The laſt Diſcouery of the

ages haue béene manned foꝛth with better Sea-men generally in reſpect of our ſmall number.

Sunday the next day, being the firſt of Apꝛill, by ſire
a clockꝭ in the moꝛning we were ſire leagues South-
South-Eaſt from the Lizarde.

Sounding.

At two a clocke in the afternœne this day, the weather
being very faire, our Captaine foꝛ his owne experience
and others with him ſounded, and had ſire and ſiftie fathoms and a halfe. The ſounding was ſome ſmall blacke
perrie ſand, ſome reddiſh ſand, a match oꝛ two, with
ſmall ſhels called Saint Iames his Shels.

**We fell with
the Ilands of
Azores.**

The foureteenth of Apꝛill being Sunday, betwéene
nine and ten of the clocke in the moꝛning our Captaine
deſcried the Iland Cueruo: which bare South-Weſt and
by Weſt, about ſeuen leagues from vs: by eleuen of the
clocke we deſcried Flores to the Southward of Cueruo,
as it lieth: by foure a clocke in the afternœne we bꝛought
Cueruo due South from vs within two leagues of the
ſhoꝛe, but we touched not, becauſe the winde was faire,
and we thought our ſelues ſufficiently watered and
wœded.

Héere our Captaine obſerued the Sunne, and found
himſelfe in the latitude of 40 degrées and 7 minutes: ſo
he iudged the Noꝛth part of Cueruo to be in 40 degrées.

After we had kept our courſe about a hundꝛed leagues
from the Ilands, by continuall Southerly windes we
were foꝛced and dꝛiuen from the Southward, whither
we firſt intended. And when our Captaine by long bea-
ting ſaw it was but in vaine to ſtriue with windes, not
knowing Gods purpoſes héerein to our further bleſſing,
(which after by his eſpeciall direction wé found) he
thought beſt to ſtand as nigh as he could by the winde to
recouer what land we might firſt diſcouer.

Sunday, the 6 of May, being in the latitude of 39 and
a halfe about ten a clocke afoꝛe nœne, we came to a riplin,
which we diſcerned a head our ſhip, which is a bꝛeach of
water cauſed either by a fall, oꝛ by ſome mœting of cur-
rents,

rents, which we iudged this to be; for the weather being very faire, and a small gale of winde, we sounded and found no ground in a hundred fathoms.

Munday, the 13 of May, about eleuen a clocke afore noone, our Captaine, iudging we were not farre from land, sounded, and had a soft oaze in a hundred and sixty fathomes. At fowre a clocke after noone we sounded againe, and had the same oaze in a hundred fathoms.

From 10 a clocke that night till three a clocke in the morning, our Captaine tooke in all sailes and lay at hull, being desirous to fall with the land in the day time, because it was an vnknowen coast, which it pleased God in his mercy to grant vs, otherwise we had run our ship vpon the hidden rockes and perished all. For when we set saile we sounded in 100 fathoms: and by eight a clock, hauing not made aboue fiue or six leagues, our Captaine vpon a sudden change of water (supposing verily he saw the sand) presently sounded, and had but fiue fathoms. Much maruelling because we saw no land, he sent one to the top, who thence descried a whitish sandy cliffe, which bare West-North-West about six leagues off from vs: but comming nærer within three or fowre leagues, we saw many breaches still nærer the land : at last we espied a great breach a head vs al along the shore, into which before we should enter, our Captaine thought best to hoise out his ship boate and sound it. Which if he had not done, we had bæne in great danger : for he bare vp the ship, as nære as he durst after the boate ; vntill Thomas Cam, his mate, being in the boat, called to him to tacke about & stand off, for in this breach he had very showld water, two fathoms and lesse vpon rockes, and sometime they supposed they saw the rocke within three or fowre foote, whereon the sea made a very strong breach : which we might discerne (from the top) to run along as we sailed by it 6 or 7 leagues to the Southward. This was in the latitude of 41 degrees , 20 minuts : wherefore we were constrained to put backe againe from the land : and soun-

ding,

ding, (the weather being very faire and a ſmall winde)
we found our ſelues embaied with continuall ſhowldes
and rockes in a moſt vncertaine ground, from fiue o2 ſixe
fathoms, at the next caſt of the lead we ſhould haue 15 &
18 fathoms. Ouer many which we paſſed, and God ſo
bleſſed vs, that we had wind and weather as faire as
poo2e men in this diſtreſſe could wiſh : whereby we both
perfectly diſcerned euery b2each, and with the winde
were able to turne, where we ſaw moſt hope of ſafeſt paſ-
ſage. Thus we parted from the land, which we had not
ſo much befo2e deſired, and at the firſt ſight reioiced, as
now we all ioifully p2aiſed God, that it had pleaſed him
to deliuer vs from ſo imminent danger.

Heere we found great ſto2e of excellent Cod fiſh, and
ſaw many Whales, as we had done two o2 th2ee daies
befo2e.

We ſtood off all that night, and the next day being
Wedneſday ; but the wind ſtill continuing betwéen the
points of South-South-Weſt, and Weſt-South-Weſt:
ſo as we could not make any way to the Southward, in
regard of our great want of water and wood (which was
now ſpent) we much deſired land, and therefo2e ſought
fo2 it, where the wind would beſt ſuffer vs to refreſh our
ſelues.

Thurſday, the 16 of May, we ſtood in directly with the
land, and much maruelled we deſcried it not, wherein
we found our ſea charts very falſe, putting land where
none is.

Friday, the 17 of May, about ſixe a clocke at night we
deſcried the land, which bare from vs No2th-No2th-
Eaſt; but becauſe it blew a great gale of winde, the ſea
very high, and néere night, not fit to come vpon an vnknowen coaſt, we ſtood off till two a clocke in the mo2-
ning, being Saturday : then ſtanding in with it againe,
we deſcried it by eight a clocke in the mo2ning, bearing
No2th-Eaſt from vs. It appeared a meane high land,
as we after found it, being but an Iland of ſome ſix miles

*The deſcrip-
tion of the
Iland.*

in

in compaſſe, but I hope the moſt foꝛtunate euer yet diſcouered. About twelue a clocke that day, we came to an
anker on the Noꝛth ſide of this Iland, about a league
from the ſhoꝛe. About two a clocke our Captaine with
twelue men rowed in his ſhip boat to the ſhoꝛe, where
we made no long ſtay, but laded our boat with dꝛy wood
of olde trees vpon the ſhoꝛe ſide, and returned to our ſhip,
where we rode that night.

This Iland is woody, growen with Firre, Birch, Oke
and Beech, as farre as we ſaw along the ſhoꝛe; and ſo
likely to be within. On the verge grow Goſeberries,
Strawberries, Wild peaſe, and Wild-roſe buſhes. The
water iſſued foꝛth downe the Rocky cliffes in many places: and much ſowle of diuers kinds bꝛæd vpon the ſhoꝛe
and rocks.

While we were at ſhoꝛe, our men aboꝛd with a few
hooks got aboue thirty great Cods and Hadocks, which
gaue vs a taſte of the great plenty of fiſh which we found
afterward whereſoeuer we went vpon the coaſt.

From hence we might diſcerne the maine land from
the Weſt-South-Weſt to the Eaſt-Noꝛth-Eaſt, and a
great way (as it then ſeemed, and as we after found it)
vp into the maine we might diſcerne very high mountaines, though the maine ſeemed but low land; which
gaue vs a hope it would pleaſe God to direct vs to the
diſcouerie of ſome good; although wee were dꝛiuen by
winds farre from that place, whither (both by our direct-
on and deſire) we euer intended to ſhape the courſe of our
voyage.

The next day, being Whit-Sunday; becauſe we rode
too much open to the ſea and windes, we weyed anker a-
bout twelue a clocke, and came along to the other Ilands
moꝛe adioyning to the maine, and in the rode directly
with the mountaines, about thꝛee leagues from the firſt
Iland where we had ankered.

When we came neere vnto them (ſounding all along

in a good depth) our Captaine manned his ſhip-boat and
ſent her before with Thomas Cam one of his Mates,
whom he knew to be of good experience, to ſound & ſearch
betwéene the Ilands for a place ſafe for our ſhippe to ride
in; in the meane while we kept alœfe at ſea, hauing giuen
them in the boat a token to weffe in the ſhip, if he found a
conuenient Harbour ; which it pleaſed God to ſend vs,
farre beyond our expectation, in a moſt ſafe birth defen=
ded from all windes, in an excellent depth of water for
ſhips of any burthen, in ſix, ſeuen, eight, nine, and ten fa=
thoms vpon a clay oaze very tough.

We all with great ioy praiſed God for his vnſpeaka
ble goodneſſe, who had from ſo apparent danger deliuered
vs, & directed vs vpon this day into ſo ſecure an Harbour:

Whitſunday. in remembrance wherot we named it Pentecoſt-harbor,
we arriuing there that day out of our laſt Harbor in England, from whence we ſet ſaile vpon Eaſterday.

About foure a clocke, after we were ankered and well
mored, our Captaine with halfe a dozen of our Company
went on ſhore to ſéeke freſh watering, and a conuenient
place to ſet together a pinneſſe, which we brought in pie=
ces out of England : both which we found very fitting.

Upon this Iland, as alſo vpon the former, we found (at
our firſt comming to ſhore) where fire had béene made :
and about the place were very great egge ſhelles bigger
than gooſe egges, fiſh bones, and as we iudged, the bones
of ſome beaſt.

Cranes. Héere we eſpied Cranes ſtalking on the ſhore of a little
Iland adioyning ; where we after ſaw they vſed to bréd.

Whitſun-munday, the 20 day of May, very early in
the morning, our Captaine cauſed the pieces of the pin=
neſſe to be carried a ſhore, where while ſome were buſied
about her, others digged welles to receiue the freſh wa=
ter, which we found iſſuing downe out of the land in ma=
ny places. Héere I can not omit (for foliſh feare of im=
putation of flattery) the painfull induſtry of our Cap=
taine

taine, who as at sea he is alwayes most carefull and vigilant, so at land he refuseth no paines; but his labour was euer as much or rather more than any mans: which not only encourageth others with better content, but also effecteth much with great expedition.

In digging we found excellent clay for bricke or tile.

The next day we finished a well of good and holesome cléere water in a great empty caske, which we left there. We cut yards, waste trées, and many necessaries for our ship, while our Carpenter and Cooper laboured to fit and furnish forth the shallop.

This day our boat went out about a mile from our ship, and in small time with two or thrée hooks was fished sufficiently for our whole Company thrée dayes, with great Cod, Haddocke, and Thornebacke.

We fished.

And towards night we drew with a small net of twenty fathoms very nigh the shore : we got about thirty very good and great Lobsters, many Rockfish, some Plaise, and other small fishes, and fishes called Lumpes, verie pleasant to the taste : and we generally obserued, that all the fish, of what kinde soeuer we tooke, were well fed, fat, and swéet in taste.

Abundance of many good fishes.

Wednesday, the 22 of May, we felled and cut wood for our ships vse, cleansed and scoured our wels, and digged a plot of ground, wherein, amongst some garden séeds, we sowed peaze and barley, which in sixtéen dayes grew eight inches aboue ground ; and so continued growing euery day halfe an inch, although this was but the crust of the ground, and much inferior to the mould we after found in the maine.

Corne sowed.

Friday, the 24 of May, after we had made an end of cutting wood, and carying water aboord our shippe, with fouretéene Shot and Pikes we marched about and thorow part of two of the Ilands ; the bigger of which we iudged to be foure or fiue miles in compasse, and a mile broad.

The

The pꝛofits and fruits which are naturally on theſe
Ilands are theſe :

The fruits of the Ilands.

All along the ſhoꝛe and ſome
ſpace within, where the
wood hindereth not, grow
plentifully

- Raſberries.
- Gooſeberries.
- Strawberries.
- Roſes.
- Currants.
- Wild-vines.
- Angelica.

Within the Ilands growe
wood of ſundꝛy ſoꝛts, ſome
very great, and all tall:

- Birch.
- Béech.
- Aſh.
- Maple.
- Spꝛuce.
- Cherry-tree.
- Yew.
- Oke very great and good.
- Firre-tree, out of which

iſſueth Turpentine in ſo maruellous plenty, and ſo ſwéet,
as our Chirurgeon and others affirmed they neuer ſaw
ſo good in England. We pulled off much Gumme congea-
led on the outſide of the barke, which ſmelled like Frank-
Incenſe. This would be a great benefit foꝛ making
Tarrs and Pitch.

We ſtayed the longer in this place, not only becauſe of
our good Harbour (which is an excellent comfoꝛt) but becauſe euery day we did moꝛe and moꝛe diſcouer the pleaſant fruitfulneſſe; inſomuch as many of our Companie
wiſhed themſelues ſetled héere, not expecting any further
hopes, oꝛ better diſcouery to be made.

Pearle.

Héere our men found abundance of great muſcels a-
mong the rocks; and in ſome of them many ſmall Pearls:
and in one muſcell (which we dꝛew vp in our net) was
found fouretéene Pearles, whereof one of pꝛety bigneſſe
and oꝛient: in another aboue fiftie ſmall Pearles: and if
we

we had had a D2ag, no doubt we had found some of great
valew, séeing these did certainly shew, that héere they
were b2ed: the shels all glittering with mother of Pearle.

Wednesday, the 29 day, our shallop being now finished, and our Captaine and men furnished to depart with
hir from the ship: we set vp a crosse on the sho2e side vpon
the rockes.

A Crosse
erected.

Thursday, the 30 of May, about ten a clock afo2e noon,
our Captaine with 13 men mo2e, in the name of God,
and with all our p2aiers fo2 their p2osperous discouerie,
and safe returne, departed in the shallop: leauing the ship
in a good harbour, which befo2e I mentioned, well mo2ed,
and manned with 14 men.

This day, about fiue a clocke in the afternoone, we in
the shippe espied th2ée Canoas comming towards vs,
which went to the iland adioining, where they went a
sho2e, and very quickly had made a fire, about which
they stood beholding our ship: to whom we made signes
with our hands and hats, wessing vnto them to come
vnto vs, because we had not séene any of the people yet.
They sent one Canoa with th2ée men, one of which,
when they came néere vnto vs, spake in his language
very lowd and very boldly: séeming as though he would
know why we were there, and by pointing with his oare
towards the sea, we coniectured he ment we should be
gone. But when we shewed them kniues and their vse,
by cutting of stickes and other trifles, as combs and glasses, they came close aboard our ship, as desirous to enter-
taine our friendship. To these we gaue such things as
we perceiued they liked, when wée shewed them the vse:
b2acelets, rings, peacocke-feathers, which they stucke
in their haire, and Tabacco pipes. After their departure
to their company on the sho2e, p2esently came foure o-
ther in another Canoa: to whom we gaue as to the fo2-
mer, vsing them with as much kindnes as we could.

The Saluages
came first to
vs.

The shape of their body is very p2opo2tionable, they
are wel countenanced, not very tal no2 big, but in stature

B 3   like

Three ſorts
of colours
of painting.

like to vs : they paint their bodies with blacke, their faces, ſome with red, ſome with blacke, and ſome with blew.

Their clothing and
buskins.

Their clothing is Beauers ſkins, or Deares ſkins, caſt ouer them like a mantle, and hanging downe to their knees, made faſt together vpon the ſhoulder with leather: ſome of them had ſleues, moſt had none : ſome had buskins of ſuch leather tewed : they haue beſides a peece of Beauers ſkin betweene their legs, made faſt about their waſte, to couer their priuities.

They ſuffer no haire to grow on their faces, but on their head very long and very blacke, which thoſe that haue wiues, binde vp behinde with a leather ſtring, in a long round knot.

They ſeemed all very ciuill and merrie : ſhewing tokens of much thankefulneſſe, for thoſe things we gaue them. We found them then (as after) a people of excæding good inuention, quicke vnderſtanding and readie capacitie.

Their boats.

Their Canoas are made without any iron, of the bark of a birch tree, ſtrengthened within with ribs and hoops of wood, in ſo good faſhion, with ſuch excellent ingenious art, as they are able to beare ſeuen or eight perſons, far excæding any in the Indies.

One of their Canoas came not to vs, wherein we imagined their women were : of whom they are (as all Saluages) very iealous.

When I ſigned vnto them they ſhould goe ſleepe, becauſe it was night, they vnderſtood preſently, and pointed that at the ſhore, right againſt our ſhip, they would ſtay all night : as they did.

The next morning very early, came one Canoa abord vs againe with three Saluages, whom we eaſily then enticed into our ſhip, and vnder the decke : where we gaue them porke, fiſh, bread and peaſe, all which they did eat : and this I noted, they would eat nothing raw, either fiſh or fleſh. They maruelled much and much looked

ked vpon the making of our canne and kettle, so they did
at a head-péece and at our guns, of which they are most
fearefull, and would fall flat downe at the report of them.
At their departure I signed vnto them, that if they would
bring me such skins as they ware I would giue them
kniues, and such things as I saw they most liked, which
the chiefe of them promised to do by that time the Sunne
should be beyond the middest of the firmament; this I did
to bring them to an vnderstanding of exchange, and that
they might conceiue the intent of our comming to them
to be for no other end.

About 10 a clocke this day we descried our Shallop
returning toward vs, which so soone as we espied, we
certainly coniectured our Captaine had found some vnex-
pected harbour, further vp towards the maine to bring
the ship into, or some riuer; knowing his determination
and resolution, not so suddenly else to make return: which
when they came néerer they expressed by shooting vol-
leies of shot; and when they were come within Musket
shot, they gaue vs a volley and haled vs, then we in
the shippe gaue them a great péece and haled them.

Thus we welcomed them, who gladded vs excéeding-
ly with their ioifull relation of their happie discouerie,
which shall appeare in the sequele. And we likewise
gaue them cause of mutuall ioy with vs, in discoursing of
the kinde ciuility we found in a people, where we little
expected any sparke of humanity.

Our Captaine had in this small time discouered vp a
great riuer, trending alongst into the maine about forty
miles. The pleasantnesse whereof, with the safety of
harbour for shipping, together with the fertility of ground
and other fruits, which were generally by his whole
company related, I omit, till I report of the whole disco-
uery therein after performed. For by the breadth, depth
and strong flood, imagining it to run far vp into the land,
he with spéed returned, intending to flanke his light hors-
man for arrowes, least it might happen that the further
part

part of the riuer ſhould be narrow, and by that meanes ſubiect to the volley of Saluages on either ſide out of the woods.

Untill his returne, our Captaine left on ſhoare where he landed in a path (which ſeemed to be frequented) a pipe, a brooch and a knife, thereby to know if the Saluages had recourſe that way, becauſe they could at that time ſee none of them, but they were taken away before our returne thither.

I returne now to our Saluages, who according to their appointment about one a clocke, came with 4 Canoas to the ſhoare of the iland right ouer againſt vs, where they had lodged the laſt night, and ſent one Canoa to vs with two of thoſe Saluages, who had beene abord, and another, who then ſeemed to haue command of them: for though we perceiued their willingneſſe, yet he would not permit them to come abord : but he hauing viewed vs and our ſhip, ſigned that he would go to the reſt of the company and returne againe. Preſently after their departure it began to raine, and continued all that afternoone, ſo as they could not come to vs with their ſkins and furs, nor we go to them. But after an howre or there about, the three which had beene with vs before came againe, whom we had to our fire and couered them with our gownes. Our Captaine beſtowed a ſhirt vpon him, whom we thought to be their chiefe, who ſeemed neuer to haue ſeene any before ; we gaue him a brooch to hang about his necke, a great knife, and leſſer kniues to the two other, and to euery one of them a combe and glaſſe, the vſe whereof we ſhewed them : whereat they laughed and tooke gladly; we victualled them, and gaue them aqua vitæ, which they taſted, but would by no meanes drinke; our beueridge they liked well, we gaue them Sugar Candy, which after they had taſted they liked and deſired more, and raiſons which were giuen them ; and ſome of euery thing they would reſerue to carry to their company. Wherefore we pittying their being in the raine, and

therefore

Trifles left on ſhore.

therefoze not able to get themselues victuall (as we thought) we gaue them bzead and fish.

Thus becaufe we found the land a place anfwereable to the intent of our difcouery, viz. fit foz any nation to inhabit, we bfed the people with as great kindnes as we could deuife, oz found them capable of. The intent of our kind vfage of the Saluages.

The next day, being Saturday and the firft of June, I traded with the Saluages all the foze-noone vpon the shoze, where were eight and twenty of them: and becaufe our ship rode nigh, we were but fiue oz fixe : where foz kniues, glaffes, combes and other trifles to the valew of foure oz fiue shillings, we had 40 god Bea uers skins, Otters skins, Sables, and other small skins, which we knewe not how to call. Our trade being ended, many of them came aboz vs, and did eat by our fire, and would be verie merrie and bold, in regard of our kinde vfage of them. Towards night our Captaine went on shoze, to haue a dzaught with the Sein oz Net. And we carried two of them with vs, who maruelled to fee vs catch fish with a net. Moft of that we caught we gaue them and their company. Then on the shoze I learned the names of diuers things of them : and when they perceiued me to note them downe, they would of themfelues, fetch fishes, and fruit bushes, and stand by me to fee me wzite their names. We traded with the Saluages.

Our Captaine shewed them a strange thing which they woondzed at. His fwozd and mine hauing bæne touched with the Loadftone, toke vp a knife, and held it faft when they pluckd it away, made the knife turne, being laid on a blocke, and touching it with his fwozd, made that take vp a nædle, whereat they much maruelled. This we did to caufe them to imagine fome great power in vs : and foz that to loue and feare vs.

When we went on shoze to trade with them, in one of their Canoas I faw their bowes and arrowes, which I toke vp and dzew an arrow in one of them, which I found to be of strength able to carry an arrow fiue oz fixe Their Bowes and Arrowes.

C fcoze

ſcoze ſtronglie : and one of them tooke it and dzew as we
dzaw our bowes, not like the Indians. Their bow is
made of Wich Hazell, and ſome of Beech in faſhion much

Their Bowes. like our bowes, but they want nocks, onely a ſtring of
Arrowes. leather put thzough a hole at one end, and made faſt with
a knot at the other. Their arrowes are made of the ſame
wood, ſome of Aſh, big and long, with thzée feathers tied
on, and nocked very artificiallie : headed with the long
ſhanke bone of a Déere, made very ſharpe with two
fangs in manner of a harping iron. They haue likewiſe
Their Darts. Darts, headed with like bone, one of which J darted a-
mong the rockes, and it bzake not. Theſe they vſe very
cunningly, to kill fiſh, fowle and beaſts.

Our Captaine had two of them at ſupper with vs in
his cabbin to ſée their demeanure, and had them in pze-
ſence at ſeruice : who behaued themſelues very ciuilly,
neither laughing noz talking all the time, and at ſupper
fed not like men of rude education, neither would they
eat oz dzinke moze than ſéemed to content nature ; they
deſired peaſe to carry a ſhoze to their women, which we
gaue them, with fiſh and bzead, and lent them pewter
diſhes, which they carefully bzought againe.

Jn the euening another boat came to them on the
Tabacco ſhoze, and becauſe they had ſome Tabacco, which they
excellent. bzought foz their owne vſe, the other came foz vs, making
ſigne what they had, and offered to carry ſome of vs in
their boat, but foure oz fiue of vs went with them in our
owne boat: when we came on ſhoze they gaue vs the beſt
welcome they could, ſpzeading fallow Déeres ſkins foz
vs to ſit on the ground by their fire, and gaue vs of their
Tabacco in our pipes, which was excellent, and ſo generally commended of vs all to be as good as any we euer
tooke, being the ſimple leafe without any compoſition,
ſtrong, and of ſwéet taſte : they gaue vs ſome to carry to
our Captaine, whom they called our Baſhabes: neither
did they require any thing foz it, but we would not receiue any thing from them without remuneration.

Héere

Héere we saw foure of their women, who stood behind
them, as desirous to sée vs, but not willing to be séene:for
before, whensoeuer we came on shore, they retired into
the woods, whether it were in regard of their owne naturall modestie, being couered only as the men with the
foresaid Beauers skins, or by the commanding iealously
of their husbands, which we rather suspected, because it
is an inclination much noted to be in Saluages; wherfore
we would by no meanes séeme to take any speciall notice
of them. They were very well fauoured in proportion
of countenance, though coloured blacke, low of stature,
and fat, bare headed as the men, wearing their haire
long: they had two little male children of a yéere and halfe
old, as we iudged, very fat and of good countenances,
which they loue tenderly, all naked, except their legs,
which were couered with thin leather buskins sewed, fastened with strops to a girdle about their waste, which
they girde very streight, and is decked round about with
little round péeces of red Copper; to these I gaue chaines
and bracelets, glasses, and other trifles, which the Saluages seemed to accept in great kindnesse.

The description of their Women and Children.

At our comming away, we would haue had those two
that supped with vs, to go aboad and sléepe, as they had
promised: but it appeared their company would not suf-
fer them. Whereat we might easily perceiue they were
much gréeued: but not long after our departure, they
came with thrée more to our ship, signing to vs, that if
one of our company would go lie on shore with them, they
would stay with vs. Then Owen Griffin (one of the two
we were to leaue in the Country, if we had thought it
néedfull or conuenient) went with them in their Canoa,
and 3 of them staied aboad vs, whom our whole company very kindly vsed. Our Captaine saw their lodging
prouided, and them lodged in an old saile vpon the Orlop;
and because they much feared our dogs, they were tied
vp whensoeuer any of them came aboad vs.

Owen Griffin, which lay on the shore, reported vnto

C 2   me

The ceremo-
nies of ỹ Sal-
uages in their
idolatry.

me their maner, and (as I may terme them) the ceremo-
nies of their idolatry: which they perfo2me thus. One a-
mong them (the eldeſt of the Company, as he iudged) riſeth right vp, the other ſitting ſtill, and looking about, ſuddenly cried with a loud voice, Baugh, Waugh: then the
women fall downe, and lie vpon the ground, and the men
all together anſwering the ſame, fall a ſtamping round a-
bout the fire with both fæt, as hard as they can, making
the ground ſhake, with ſund2y out-cries, and change of
voice and ſound. Many take the fire-ſticks and th2uſt
them into the earth, and then reſt awhile: of a ſudden be-
ginning as befo2e, they continue ſo ſtamping, till the yon-
ger ſo2t fetched from the ſho2e many ſtones, of which euery man tooke one, and firſt beat vpon them with their fire
ſticks, then with the ſtones beat the earth with all their
ſtrength. And in this maner (as he repo2ted) they continued aboue two houres.

They lie with
their wiues
ſecretly.

After this ended, they which haue wiues take them a-
part, and withd2aw themſelues ſeuerally into the wood
all night.

The next mo2ning, aſſoone as they ſaw the Sunne riſe,
they pointed to him to come with them to our ſhippe: and
hauing receiued their men from vs, they came with fiue
o2 ſixe of their Canoas and Company houering about our
ſhip: to whom (becauſe it was the Sabbath day) I ſigned
they ſhould depart, and at the next Sun riſing we would
goe along with them to their houſes: which they vnderſtood (as we thought) and departed, ſome of their Canoas
courſing about the Iland, and the other directly towards
the maine.

This day, about fiue a clocke after noone, came th2ée
other Canoas from the maine, of which ſome had bæne
with vs befo2e; and they came abo02d vs, and b2ought vs
Tabacco, which we tooke with them in their pipes, which
were made of earth, very ſtrong, blacke, and ſho2t, contai-
ning a great quantity: ſome Tabacco they gaue vnto our
Captaine, and ſome to me, in very ciuill kind maner. We
requited

North part of *Virginia*.

requited them with bread and peaze, which they caried to
their Company on shore, seeming very thankefull. After
supper they returned with their Canoa to fetch vs a shore
to take Tabacco with them there; with whom six or seuen
of vs went, and caried some trifles, if peraduenture they
had any trucke, among which I caried some few biskets,
to try if they would exchange for them, seeing they so well
liked to eat them. When we came at shore, they most
kindly entertained vs, taking vs by the hands, as they had
obserued we did to them aboord, in token of welcome, and
brought vs to sitdowne by their fire, where sat together
thirteene of them. They filled their Tabacco pipe, which
was then the short claw of a Lobster, which will hold ten
of our pipes full, and we dranke of their excellent Tabacco as much as we would with them; but we saw not any
great quantity to trucke for; and it seemed they had not
much left of old, for they spend a great quantity yeerely by
their continuall drinking: and they would signe vnto vs,
that it was growen yet but a foot aboue ground and would
be aboue a yard high, with a leafe as broad as both their
hands. They often would (by pointing to one part of the
maine Eastward) signe vnto vs, that their Bashabes (that
is, their King) had great plenty of Furres, and much Tabacco. When we had sufficiently taken Tabacco with
them, I shewed some of our trifles for trade; but they
made signe that they had there nothing to exchange; for
(as I after conceiued) they had beene fishing and fowling,
and so came thither to lodge that night by vs: for when
we were ready to come away, they shewed vs great cups
made very wittily of barke, in forme almost square, full of
a red berry about the bignesse of a bullis, which they did
eat, and gaue vs by handfuls; of which (though I liked
not the taste) yet I kept some, because I would by no
meanes but accept their kindnesse. They shewed me likewise a great piece of fish, whereof I tasted, and it was fat
like Porpoise; and another kinde of great scaly fish, broi-
led on the scales, much like white Salmon, which the

The dwelling of Bashabes is Eastward from ye great Riuer.

A red berrie which they feede on.

C 3   Frenchmen

Frenchmen call Aloza, foz theſe they would haue had bzead; which I refuſed, becauſe in maner of exchange, I would alwayes make the greateſt eſtæme I could of our commodities whatſoeuer; although they ſaw abozd our Captaine was liberall to giue them, to the end we might allure them ſtill to frequent vs. Then they ſhewed me foure yong Goſlings, foz which they required foure biſkets, but I offered them two; which they tœke and were well content.

We had yong Goſlings of the Saluages.

At our departure they made ſigne, that if any or vs would ſtay there on ſhoze, ſome of them would go lie abozd vs: at which motion two of our Company ſtayed with them, and thzée of the Saluages lodged with vs in maner as the night befoze.

Iune 3.

Early the next mozning, being Munday the third of Iune, when they had bzought our men abozd, they came about our ſhip, earneſtly by ſignes deſiring that we would go with them along to the maine, foz that there they had Furres and Tabacco to traffique with vs. Wherefoze our Captaine manned the light-hozſeman with as many men as he could well, which were about fiftéene with rowers and all; and we went along with them. Two of their Canoas they ſent away befoze, and they which lay abozd vs all night, kept company with vs to direct vs.

Their Canoa outrowed vs.

This we noted as we went along, they in their Canoa with thzée oares, would at their will go ahead of vs and about vs, when we rowed with eight oares ſtrong; ſuch was their ſwiftneſſe, by reaſon of the lightneſſe and artificiall compoſition of their Canoa and oares.

When we came nære the point where we ſaw their fires, where they intended to land, and where they imagined ſome few of vs would come on ſhoze with our merchandize, as we had accuſtomed befoze; when they had often numbzed our men very diligently, they ſcoured away to their Campany, not doubting we would haue followed them. But when we perceiued this, and knew not either their intents, or number of Saluages on the ſhoze; our ſo good deepes, our Captaine to make ſome triall of the fiſhing himſelfe, cauſed a hooke or two to be caſt out at the mouth of the harbour, not aboue halfe a league from our ſhip, where in ſmall time only, with the baits which they cut from the fiſh and three hooks, we got fiſh enough for our whole Company (though now augmented) for three daies. Which I omit not to report, becauſe it ſheweth how great a profit the fiſhing would be, they being ſo plentifull, ſo great, and ſo good, with ſuch conuenient drying as can be wiſhed, neere at hand vpon the Rocks.

This day, about one a clocke after noone, came from the Eaſtward two Canoas abord vs, wherein was he that refuſed to ſtay with vs for a pawne, and with him ſix other Saluages which we had not ſeene before, who had beautified themſelues after their manner very gallantly, though their clothing was not differing from the former, yet they had newly painted their faces very deep, ſome all blacke, ſome red, with ſtripes of excellent blew ouer their vpper lips, noſe and chin. One of them ware a kinde of Coronet about his head, made very cunningly, of a ſubſtance like ſtiffe haire coloured red, broad, and more then a handfull in depth, which we imagined to be ſome enſigne of his ſuperioritie: for he ſo much eſteemed it as he would not for any thing exchange the ſame. Other ware the white feathered ſkins of ſome fowle, round about their head, iewels in their eares, and bracelets of little white round bone, faſtned together vpon a leather ſtring. Theſe made not any ſhew that they had notice of the other beforetaken, but we vnderſtood them by their ſpeech and ſignes, that they came ſent from the Baſhabes, and that his deſire was that we would bring vp our ſhip (which they call as their owne boats, a Quiden) to his houſe, being, as they pointed, vpon the main towards the Eaſt, from whence they came, and that he would exchange with vs for Furres and Tabacco. But becauſe our Company was but ſmall, and now our deſire was with ſpeed to diſcouer vp the riuer, we let them vnderſtand,

ſtand,

our Captaine, after conſultation, ſtood off, and wefted them to vs, determining that I ſhould go on ſhore firſt to take a view of them, and what they had to traffique: if he, whom at our firſt ſight of them ſeemed to be of moſt reſpect among them, and being then in the Canoa, would ſtay as a pawne for me. When they came to vs (notwithſtanding all our former courteſies) he vtterly refuſed; but would leaue a yong Saluage: and for him our Captaine ſent Griffin in their Canoa, while we lay hulling a little off. Griffin at his returne reported, they had there aſſembled together, as he numbred them, two hundred eighty three Saluages, euery one his bowe and arrowes, with their dogges, and wolues which they keepe tame at command, and not any thing to exchange at all; but would haue drawen vs further vp into a little narrow nooke of a riuer, for their Furres, as they pretended. *283 Saluages.*

Theſe things conſidered, we began to ioyne them in the ranke of other Saluages, who haue beene by trauellers in moſt diſcoueries found very trecherous: neuer attempting miſchiefe, vntill by ſome remiſneſſe, fit opportunity affordeth them certaine ability to execute the ſame. Wherefore after good aduice taken, we determined ſo ſoone as we could to take ſome of them, leaſt (being ſuſpitious we had diſcouered their plots) they ſhould abſent themſelues from vs.

Tueſday, the fourth of June, our men tooke Cod and Hadocke with hooks by our ſhip ſide, and Lobſters very great: which before we had not tried. *Fiſh in the Harbour.*

About eight a clocke this day we went on ſhore with our boats, to fetch abord water and wood, our Captaine leauing word with the Gunner in the ſhippe, by diſcharging a muſket, to giue notice if they eſpied any Canoa comming: which they did about ten a clocke. He therefore being carefull they ſhould be kindly entreated, requeſted me to go abord, intending with diſpatch to make what haſte after he poſſibly could. When I came to the ſhip, there were two Canoas, and in either of them three Saluages.

Saluages ; of whom two were below at the fire, the other ſtaied in their Canoas about the ſhip ; and becauſe we could not entice them aboʒd, we gaue them a Canne of peaſe and bʒead, which they carried to the ſhoʒe to eat. But one of them bʒought backe our Canne pʒeſently and ſtaid aboʒd with the other two ; foʒ he being yœng, of a ready capacity, and one we moſt deſired to bʒing with vs into England, had recciued excœding kinde vſage at our hands, and was therefoʒe much delighted in our company. When our Captaine was come, we conſulted how to catch the other thʒœ at ſhoʒe, which we perfoʒmed thus.

Our manner of taking the Saluages.

We manned the light hoʒſeman with 7 oʒ 8 men, one ſtanding befoʒe carried our box of Marchandiſe, as we were wœnt when I went to traffique with them, and a platter of peaſe, which meat they loued : but befoʒe we were landed, one of them (being tœ ſuſpitiouſly fearefull of his owne gœd) withdʒew himſelfe into the wœd. The other two met vs on the ſhoʒe ſide, to receiue the peaſe, with whom we went vp the Cliffe to their fire and ſate downe with them, and whiles we were diſcuſſing how to catch the third man who was gone, I opened the box, and ſhewed them trifles to exchange, thinking thereby to haue baniſht feare from the other, and dʒawen him to returne : but when we could not, we vſed little delay, but ſuddenly laid hands vpon them. And it was as much as fiue oʒ ſixe of vs could dœ to get them into the light hoʒſeman. Foʒ they were ſtrong and ſo naked as our beſt hold was by their long haire on their heads : and we would haue bœne very loath to haue done them any hurt, which of neceſſity we had bœne conſtrained to haue dóne if we had attempted them in a multitude, which we muſt and would, rather than haue wanted them, being a matter of great impoʒtance foʒ the full accompleſment of our voyage.

We caught fiue Saluages, two Canoas, and their bowes and arrowes.

Thus we ſhipped fiue Saluages, two Canoas, with all their bowes and arrowes.

The

The next day we made an end of g__
boʒd, and filled our empty caſke with __

Thurſday, the 6 of June, we ſpen__
Canoas vpon the oʒlop ſafe from hurt, __
ſubiect to bʒeaking, which our Capta__
pʒeuent.

Saturday, the eight of June (our __
ſirous to finiſh all buſineſſe about this __
ly in the moʒning, with the light hoʒſ__
oʒ ſixe leagues about the Ilands adioi__
all along whereſoeuer we went. Vs __
ſearched the mouth of the Harbour, __
which ſhew themſelues at all times, __
bʒeach of the water, ſo as no Sea c__
the Harbour. This he did to inſtruct __
by able to direct others that ſhall hap__
place. Foʒ euery where both nœre th__
dings about the Ilands, we neuer fo__
foure and fiue fathoms, which was __
eight, nine and ten fathoms is the co__
the ſhoʒe. In ſome places much dœ__
ſoft ſand : ſo that if any bound foʒ th__
ther dʒiuen oʒ ſcanted with winds, __
his directions) to recouer ſafely his __
in water enough by foure ſeuerall __
which I thinke no man of iudg__
neceſſarie.

Upon one of the Ilands (becauſe __
by Coue foʒ ſmall barks to ride in) __
hard by the ſhoʒe a pond of freſh wa__
uer the banks, ſomewhat ouergro__
trœs, and ſearching vp in the Iland__
ſtrong run, which with ſmall la__
might be made to dʒiue a mill. In __
other, were ſpʒuce trœs of excelle__
able to maſt ſhips of great burthen __

While we thus ſounded from __

stand, that if their Bashabes would come to vs, he should be welcome, but we would not remoue to him. Which when they vnderstood (receiuing of vs bread and fish, and euery of them a knife) they departed; for we had then no will to stay them long aboord, least they should discouer the other Saluages which we had stowed below.

Tuesday, the 11 of June, we passed vp into the riuer with our ship, about six and twenty miles. Of which I had rather not write, then by my relation to detract from the worthinesse thereof. For the Riuer, besides that it is subiect by shipping to bring in all traffiques of Marchandise, a benefit alwaies accounted the richest treasury to any land : for which cause our Thames hath that one denomination, and France by her nauigable Riuers receiueth hir greatest wealth ; yet this place of it selfe from God and nature affordeth as much diuersitie of good commodities, as any reasonable man can wish, for present habitation and planting.

We went vp with our ship into the Riuer.

The first and chiefest thing required, is a bold coast and faire land to fall with ; the next, a safe harbour for ships to ride in.

The first is a speciall attribute to this shore, being most free from sands or dangerous rocks in a continuall good depth, with a most excellent land-fall, which is the first Iland we fell with, named by vs, Saint Georges Iland. For the second, by iudgement of our Captaine, who knoweth most of the coast of England, and most of other Countries, (hauing bæne experienced by imployments in discoueries and trauels from his childhood) and by opinion of others of good iudgement in our shippe, hære are more good harbours for ships of all burthens, than England can afford, and far more secure from all winds and weathers, than any in England, Scotland, France or Spaine. For besides without the Riuer in the channell, and sounds about the ilands adioining to the mouth therof, no better riding can be desired for an infinite number of ships. The Riuer it selfe as it runneth vp into the main

The profits of the Riuer.

D 2   very

The breadth of the Riuer.	very nigh forty miles toward the great mountaines, beareth in bredth a mile, ſometime three quarters, and halfe a mile is the narroweſt, where you ſhall neuer haue vnder 4 and 5 fathoms water hard by the ſhore, but 6,7,8,9, and 10 fathoms all along, and on both ſides euery halfe mile very gallant Coues, ſome able to conteine almoſt
The ground ſoft ooze and clay.	a hundred ſaile, where the ground is excellent ſoft ooze with a tough clay vnder for anker hold, and where ſhips may ly without either Cable or Anker, only mored to the ſhore with a Hauſer.
What flowe of water.	It floweth by their iudgement eighten or twenty foot at high water.
Docks to graue and carine ſhips.	Here are made by nature moſt excellent places, as Docks to graue or Carine ſhips of all burthens : ſecured from all windes, which is ſuch a neceſſary incomparable benefit, that in few places in England, or in any parts of Chriſtendome, art, with great charges, can make the like.
The Land.	Beſides, the bordering land is a moſt rich neighbour trending all along on both ſides, in an equall plaine, neither mountainous nor rocky, but verged with a grene bordure of graſſe, doth make tender vnto the beholder of hir pleaſant fertility, if by clenſing away the woods ſhe were conuerted into meddow.
The wood.	The wood ſhe beareth is not ſhrubbiſh fit only for fewell, but goodly tall Firre, Spruce, Birch, Bech, Oke, which in many places is not ſo thicke, but may with ſmall labour be made feding ground, being plentifull like the outward Ilands with freſh water, which ſtreameth downe in many places.

As we paſſed with a gentle winde vp with our ſhip in this Riuer, any man may conceiue with what admiration we all conſented in ioy. Many of our Company who had bene trauellers in ſundry countries, and in the moſt famous Riuers, yet affirmed them not comparable to this they now beheld. Some that were with Sir Walter Ralegh in his voyage to Guiana, in the diſcouery of the Riuer

uer

uer Orenoque, which echoed fame to the worlds eares, gaue reasons why it was not to be compared with this, which wanteth the dangers of many Shoules, and broken ground, wherewith that was incombred. Others before that notable Riuer in the West Indies called Rio Grande; some before the Riuer of Loyer, the Riuer Seine, and of Burdeaux in France; which although they be great and godly Riuers, yet it is no detraction from them to be accounted inferiour to this, which not only yeeldeth all the foresaid pleasant profits, but also appeared infallibly to vs free from all inconueniences. *This riuer preferred before Orenoque: and why.*

I will not prefer it before our riuer of Thames, because it is Englands richest treasure; but we all did wish those excellent Harbours, good deeps in a continuall conuenient breadth, and small tide gates, to be aswell therein for our countries good, as we found the here (beyond our hopes) in certaine, for those to whom it shall please God to grant this land for habitation; which if it had, with the other inseparable adherent commodities here to be found; then I would boldly affirme it to be the most rich, beautifull, large & secure harbouring riuer that the world affordeth.

Wednesday, the twelfth of June, our Captaine manned his light-horseman with 17 men, and ranne vp from the ship riding in the riuer vp to the codde thereof, where we landed, leauing six to keepe the light-horseman till our returne. Ten of vs with our shot, and some armed, with a boy to carry powder and match, marched vp into the countrey towards the mountaines, which we descried at our first falling with the land. Unto some of them the riuer brought vs so neere, as we iudged our selues when we landed to haue beene within a league of them: but we marched vp about foure miles in the maine, and passed ouer three hilles: and because the weather was parching hot, and our men in their armour not able to trauel farre and returne that night to our ship, we resolued not to passe any further, being all very weary of so tedious and laboursom a trauell. *We marched vp into the land about 4 miles.*

Ie.

Good paſture In this march we paſſed ouer very good ground, pleaſant and fertile, fit for paſture, for the ſpace of ſome three miles, hauing but little wood, and that Oke like ſtands left in our paſtures in England, good and great, fit timber for any vſe. Some ſmall Birch, Hazle and Brake, which might in ſmall time with few men be cleanſed and made good arable land : but as it now is will feed cattell of all kindes with fodder enough for Summer and Winter. The ſoile is blacke, bearing ſundry hearbs, graſſe, and ſtrawberries bigger than ours in England. In many places are lowe Thicks like our Copiſſes of ſmall yong wood. And ſurely it did all reſemble a ſtately Parke, wherein appeare ſome old trees with high withered tops, and other flouriſhing with liuing greene boughs. Upon the hilles grow notable high timber trees, maſts for ſhips of 400 tun : and at the bottome of euery hill, a little run of freſh water : but the furtheſt and laſt we paſſed, ranne with a great ſtreame able to driue a mill.

Deere.
Hares.
Hogges.
We might ſee in ſome places where fallow Deers and Hares had beene, and by the rooting of ground we ſuppoſed wilde Hogs had ranged there, but we could deſcrie no beaſt, becauſe our noiſe ſtill chaſed them from vs.

We were no ſooner come aboord our light-horſeman, returning towards our ſhip, but we eſpied a Canoa comming from the farther part of the Cod of the riuer Eaſtward, which haſted to vs; wherin, with two others, was he who refuſed to ſtay for a pawne : and his comming was very earneſtly importing to haue one of our men to go lie on ſhore with their Baſhabes (who was there on ſhore, as they ſigned)and then the next morning he would come to our ſhip with many Furres and Tabacco. This we perceiued to be only a meere deuice to get poſſeſſion of any of our men, to ranſome all thoſe which we had taken, which their naturall policy could not ſo ſhadow, but we did eaſily diſcouer and preuent. Theſe meanes were by this Saluage practiſed, becauſe we had one of his kinſemen priſoner, as we iudged by his moſt kinde vſage of
him

him being aboard vs together.

Thurſday, the 13 of June, by two a clocke in the morning (becauſe our Captaine would take the helpe and aduantage of the tide) in the light-horſeman with our Company well prouided and furniſhed with armour and ſhot both to defend and offend; we went from our ſhip vp to that part of the riuer which trended Weſtward into the maine, to ſearch that : and we carried with vs a Croſſe, to erect at that point, which (becauſe it was not daylight) we left on the ſhore vntill our returne backe; when we set it vp in maner as the former. For this (by the way) we diligently obſerued, that in no place, either about the Ilands, or vp in the maine, or alongſt the riuer, we could diſcerne any token or ſigne, that euer any Chriſtian had béene before; of which either by cutting wood, digging for water, or ſetting vp Croſſes (a thing neuer omitted by any Chriſtian trauellers) we ſhould haue perceiued ſome mention left.

We ſet vp another croſſe.

But to returne to our riuer, further vp into which we then rowed by eſtimation twenty miles, the beauty and goodneſſe whereof I can not by relation ſufficiently demonſtrate. That which I can ſay in generall is this: What profit or pleaſure ſoeuer is deſcribed and truly verified in the former part of the riuer, is wholly doubled in this; for the bredth and depth is ſuch, that any ſhip drawing 17 or 18 foot water, might haue paſſed as farre as we went with our light-horſman, and by all our mens iudgement much further, becauſe we left it in ſo good depth and bredth; which is ſo much the more to be eſtéemed of greater worth, by how much it trendeth further vp into the maine : for from the place of our ſhips riding in the Harbour at the entrance into the Sound, to the furtheſt part we were in this riuer, by our eſtimation was not much leſſe than thréeſcore miles.

Conueniency of tranſportation.

From ech banke of this riuer are diuers branching ſtreames into the maine, wherby is afforded an vnſpeakable profit by the conueniency of tranſportation from
place

place to place, which in ſome countries is both chargea-
ble, and not ſo fit, by cariages on waine, or horſebacke.

Héere we ſaw great ſtore of fiſh ſome great, leaping a-
boue water, which we iudged to be Salmons. All along
is an excellent mould of ground. The wood in moſt places, eſpecially on the Eaſt ſide, very thinne, chiefly oke
and ſome ſmall yong birch, bordering low vpon the riuer; all fit for medow and paſture ground : and in that
ſpace we went, we had on both ſides the riuer many
plaine plots of medow, ſome of thrée or foure acres, ſome

Meddow and
Graſſe.

of eight or nine : ſo as we iudged in the whole to be betwéene thirty and forty acres of good graſſe, and where
the armes run out into the Maine, there likewiſe went a
ſpace on both ſides of cléere graſſe, how far we know not,
in many places we might ſée paths made to come downe
to the watering.

The excellencie of this part of the Riuer, for his good
breadth, depth, and fertile bordering ground, did ſo ra-
uiſh vs all with variety of pleaſantneſſe, as we could
not tell what to commend, but only admired; ſome compared it to the Riuer Seuerne, (but in a higher degrée)
and we all concluded (as I verily thinke we might rightly) that we ſhould neuer ſée the like Riuer in euery degrée
equall, vntill it pleaſed God we beheld the ſame againe.
For the farther we went, the more pleaſing it was to e-
uery man, alluring vs ſtill with expectation of better, ſo
as our men, although they had with great labour rowed
long and eat nothing (for we carried with vs no victuall,

We were
loath to leaue
this Riuer.

but a little chéeſe and bread) yet they were ſo refreſhed
with the pleaſant beholding thereof, and ſo loath to for-
ſake it, as ſome of them affirmed, they would haue continued willingly with that onely fare and labour 2 daies;
but the tide not ſuffering vs to make any longer ſtay (becauſe we were to come backe with the tide) and our Captaine better knowing what was fit then we, and better
what they in labour were able to endure, being verie
loath to make any deſperate hazard, where ſo little neceſ-
ſitie

sitie required, thought it best to make returne, because
whither we had discouered was sufficient to conceiue
that the Riuer ran very far into the land. For we passed
sir or seuen miles, altogether fresh water (whereof we all
dranke) forced vp by the flowing of the Salt: which after
a great while eb, where we left it, by breadth of channell
and depth of water was likely to run by estimation of our
whole company an vnknowen way farther: the search
whereof our Captaine hath left till his returne, if it shall
so please God to dispose of him and vs.

For we hauing now by the direction of the omnipotent
disposer of all good intents (far beyond the period of our
hopes) fallen with so bold a coast, found so excellent and
secure harbour, for as many ships as any nation profes-
sing Christ is able to set forth to Sea, discouered a Riuer,
which the All-creating God, with his most liberall hand,
hath made aboue report notable with his foresaid bles-
sings, bordered with a land, whose pleasant fertility bewraieth it selfe to be the garden of nature, wherin she only intended to delight hir selfe, hauing hitherto obscured
it to any, except to a purblind generation, whose vnderstanding it hath pleased God so to darken, as they can
neither discerne, vse, or rightly esteeme the vnualuable
riches in middest whereof they liue sensually content
with the barke and outward rinde, as neither knowing
the sweetnes of the inward marrow, nor acknowledging
the Deity of the Almighty giuer: hauing I say thus far
proceeded, and hauing some of the inhabitant nation (of
best vnderstanding we saw among them) who (learning
our language) may be able to giue vs further instruction,
concerning all the premised particulars, as also of their
gouernours, and gouernment, situation of townes, and
what else shall be conuenient, which by no meanes otherwise we could by any obseruation of our selues learne in a
long time: our Captaine now wholy intended his pro-
uision for speedy returne. For although the time of yeere
and our victuall were not so spent, but we could haue
                    C   made

made a longer voyage, in ſearching farther and trading foz very good commodities, yet as they might haue beene much pzofitable,ſo(our company being ſmall)much moze pzeiudiciall to the whole ſtate of our voyage, which we were moſt regardfull now not to hazard. Foz we ſuppoſing not a little pzeſent pziuate pzofit, but a publique good, and true zeale of pzomulgating Gods holy Church, by planting Chziſtianity, to be the ſole intent of the Honourable ſetters foozth of this diſcouery ; thought it generally moſt expedient, by our ſpeedy returne, to giue the longer ſpace of time to make pzouiſion foz ſo weighty an enterpzife.

The cauſe of our ſpeedy returne.

Friday, the 14 day of June, early by foure a clocke in the mozning, with the tide, our two boats, and a little helpe of the winde, we rowed downe to the riuers mouth and there came to an anker about eleuen a clocke. Afterward our Captaine in the light hozſeman ſearched the ſounding all about the mouth and comming to the Riuer, foz his certaine inſtruction of a perfect deſcription.

We ankerd at the mouth of the Riuer.

The next day, being Saturday, we wayed anker, and with a bzicſe from the land, we ſailed vp to our watering place, and there ſtopped, went on ſhoze and filled all our empty caſke with freſh water.

Our Captaine vpon the Rocke in the middeſt of the harbour obſerued the height, latitude, and variation exactly vpon his inſtruments.

Our Captain made his certaine obſeruation.

1 Aſtrolabe.
2 Semiſphere.
3 Ringe inſtrument.
4 Croſſe ſtaffe.
5 And an excellent compaſſe made foz the variation.

The certainty whereof, together with the particularities of euery depth and ſounding, aſwell at our falling with the land, as in the diſcouery, and at our departure from the coaſt; I refer to his owne relation in the Map of his Geographicall deſcription, which foz the benefit of others he intendeth moſt exactly to publiſh.

The

The temperature of the Climate (albeit a very im-portant matter) I had almost passed without mentio-ning, because it afforded to vs no great alteration from our disposition in England; somwhat hotter vp into the Maine, because it lieth open to the South; the aire so wholesome, as I suppose not any of vs found our selues at any time more healthfull, more able to labour, nor with better stomacks to such good fare, as we partly brught, and partly found.

Sunday, the 16 of June, the winde being faire, and because we had set out of England vpon a Sunday, made the Ilands vpon a Sunday, and as we doubt not (by Gods appointment) happily fell into our harbour vpon a Sunday; so now (beseeching him still with like prospe-rity to blesse our returne into England our country, and from thence with his good will and pleasure to hasten our next arriuall there) we waied Anker and quit the Land vpon a Sunday.

Tuesday, the 18 day, being not run aboue 30 leagues from land, and our Captaine for his certaine knowledge how to fall with the coast, hauing sounded euery watch, and from 40 fathoms had come into good deeping, to 70, and so to an hundred : this day the weather being faire, after the foure a clocke watch, when we supposed not to haue found ground so farre from land, and before sounded in aboue 100 fathoms, we had ground in 24 fathomes. Wherefore our sailes being downe, Thomas King boat-swaine, presently cast out a hooke, and before he iudged it at ground; was fished and haled vp an exceeding great and well fed Cod: then there were cast out 3 or 4 more, and the fish was so plentifull and so great, as when our Captaine would haue set saile, we all desired him to suf-fer them to take fish a while, because we were so delight-ed to see them catch so great fish, so fast as the hooke came downe : some with playing with the hooke they tooke by the backe, and one of the Mates with two hookes at a lead at fiue draughts together haled vp tenne fishes; all

C 2   were

were generally very great, ſome they meaſured to be fiue
foot long, and thꝛee foot about.

A fiſhing
banke.

This cauſed our Captaine not to maruell at the ſhoul-
ding, foꝛ he perceiued it was a fiſh banke; which (foꝛ our
farewell from the land) it pleaſed God in continuance of
his bleſſings, to giue vs knowledge of: the abundant pꝛo-
fit whereof ſhould be alone ſufficient cauſe to dꝛaw men
againe, if there were no other good both in pꝛeſent certaine, and in hope pꝛobable to be diſcouered. To ampli-
fie this with woꝛds, were to adde light to the Sunne: foꝛ
euery one in the ſhippe could eaſily account this pꝛeſent
commodity; much moꝛe thoſe of iudgement, which knew
what belonged to fiſhing, would warrant (by the helpe
of God) in a ſhoꝛt voyage with few good fiſhers to make
a moꝛe pꝛofitable returne from hence than from New-
found-land : the fiſh being ſo much greater, better fed,
and abundant with traine; of which ſome they deſired,
and did bꝛing into England to beſtow among their
friends, and to teſtifie the true repoꝛt.

After, we kept our courſe directly foꝛ England & with
oꝛdinary winds, and ſometime calmes, vpon Sunday
the 14 of July about ſix a clocke at night, we were come

We came in-
to ſounding.

into ſounding in our channell, but with darke weather
and contrary winds, we were conſtrained to beat vp and
downe till Tueſday the 16 of July, when by fiue a clocke
in the moꝛning we made Sylly; from whence, hindered
with calmes and ſmall winds, vpon Thurſday the 18 of
July about foure a clocke after noone, we came into
Dartmouth : which Hauen happily (with Gods gracious aſſiſtance) we made our laſt and firſt Harbour in
England.

Further, I haue thought fit here to adde ſome things
woꝛthy to be regarded, which we haue obſerued from
the Saluages ſince we tooke them.

Firſt, although at the time when we ſurpꝛiſed them,
they made their beſt reſiſtance, not knowing our purpoſe,
noꝛ what we were, noꝛ how we meant to vſe them; yet
after

after perceiuing by their kinde vsage we intended them no
harme, they haue neuer since séemed discontented with vs,
but very tractable, louing, & willing by their best meanes
to satisfie vs in any thing we demand of them, by words
or signes for their vnderstanding : neither haue they at a-
ny time béene at the least discord among themselues ; in-
somuch as we haue not séene them angry, but merry ; and
so kinde, as if you giue any thing to one of them, he will
distribute part to euery one of the rest.

We haue brought them to vnderstand some English,
and we vnderstand much of their language ; so as we are
able to aske them many things. And this we haue obserued, that if we shew them any thing, and aske them if
they haue it in their countrey, they will tell you if they
haue it, and the vse of it, the difference from ours in bignesse, colour, or forme : but if they haue it not, be it a thing
neuer so precious, they wil denie the knowledge of it.

They haue names for many starres, which they will
shew in the firmament.

They shew great reuerence to their King, and are in
great subiection to their Gouernours : and they will shew
a great respect to any we tell them are our Commanders.

They shew the maner how they make bread of their
Indian wheat, and how they make butter and chéese of
the milke they haue of the Rain-Déere and Fallo-Déere,
which they haue taine as we haue Cowes.

They haue excellent colours. And hauing séene our
Indico, they make shew of it, or of some other like thing
which maketh as good a blew.

Indico and o-
ther excellent
colours in the
countrey.

One especiall thing is their maner of killing the
Whale, which they call Powdawe ; and will describe his
forme ; how he bloweth vp the water ; and that he is
12 fathoms long ; and that they go in company of their
King with a multitude of their boats, and strike him with
a bone made in fashion of a harping iron fastened to a rope,
which they make great and strong of the barke of trées,
which they beare out after him : then all their boats

Their killing
of the whale.

E 3   come

come about him, and as he riſeth aboue water, with their arrowes they ſhoot him to death: when they haue killed him & dzagged him to ſhoze, they call all their chiefe lozds together, & ſing a ſong of ioy: and thoſe chiefe lozds, whom they call Sagamos, diuide the ſpoile, and giue to euery man a ſhare, which pieces ſo diſtributed they hang vp about their houſes foz pzouiſion: and when they boile them, they blow off the fat, and put to their peaze, maiz, and other pulſe, which they eat.

A briefe Note of what profits we ſaw the Countrey yeeld in the ſmall time of our ſtay there.

T R E E S.
Oke of an excellent graine, ſtrait, and great timber.
Elme.
Beech.
Birch, very tall & great; of whoſe barke they make their Canoas.
Wich-Hazell.
Hazell.
Alder.
Cherry-tree.
Aſh.
Maple.
Yew.
Spruce.
Aſpe.
Firre.
Many fruit trees, which we knew not.

F O W L E S.
Eagles.
Hernſhawes.
Cranes.
Ducks great.
Geeſe.
Swannes.
Penguins.
Crowes.
Sharks.
Rauens.
Mewes.
Turtle-doues.
Many birds of ſundrie colours.
Many other fowls in flocks, vnknowen.

B E A S T S.
Raine-Deere.
Stagges.
Fallow-Deere.
Beares.
Wolues.
Beauer.
Otter.
Hare.

Cony,

Cony.
Hedge-Hoggs.
Polcats.
Wilde great Cats.
Dogges : fome like Wolues,
fome like Spaniels.

F I S H E S.

Whale.
Seales.
Cod very great.
Haddocke great.
Herring great.
Plaife.
Thornebacke.
Rockefifh.
Lobftar great,
Crabs.
Mufcels great, with pearles
in them.
Cockles:
Tilt.
Cunner fifh.
Lumps.
Whiting.
Soales.

Tortoifes.
Oifters.

F R V I T S, P L A N T S,
and H E R B S.

Tabacco , excellent fweet
and ftrong.
Wild Vines.
Strawberries ⎫
Rafpberries ⎪
Goofeberries ⎬abundance.
Hurtleberries ⎪
Currant trees ⎭
Rofe-bufhes.
Peaze.
Ground-nuts.
Angelica, a moft foueraigne
herbe.
An hearbe that fpreadeth
the ground , & fmelleth
like *Sweet Marioram,*
great plenty.
Very good Dies,which ap-
peare by their painting ;
which they carrie with
them in bladders.

The names of the fiue Saluages which we
brought home into *England,* which are
all yet aliue, are thefe.

1. *Taháncdo,* a Sagamo or Commander.
2. *Amóret* ⎫
3. *Skicowáros* ⎬Gentlemen.
4. *Maneddo* ⎭
5. *Saffacomoit,* a feruant.